Copyright © [2023] by Phillip and Phoenix Phunne

Dedicated to everyone who needs a good laugh. We hope this book gives you laughs to share.

My Fart Is Stuck

One sunny afternoon, Timmy was playing in his backyard, when his tummy began to rumble.

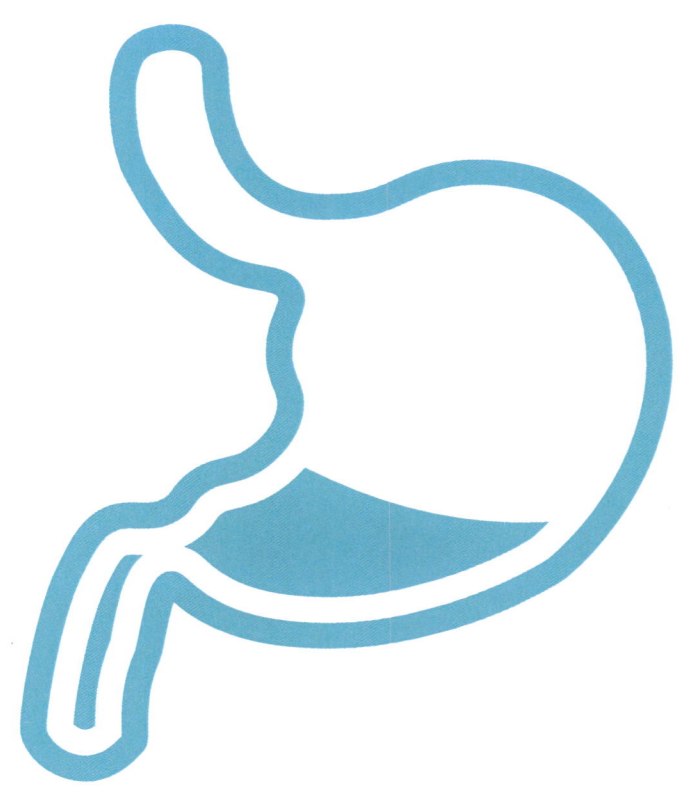

This wasn't just any ordinary rumble—it was a rumble that could only mean one thing: a powerful, room-shaking fart was about to escape!

But this fart had other plans.

It refused to come out. He tried hopping around, doing jumping jacks and even doing handstands.

Timmy knew he needed help.
So he found his Mom.

"Mom, my fart is stuck" he announced. She told him to try standing on his head.

That didn't work. So he found his Dad. He told him to eat beans.

Despite devouring a plate of beans the fart remained stubbornly stuck, causing Timmy to feel both frustrated and a little gassy.

Rumor of his stuck fart quickly spread through the family.

His sister told him to quack like a duck.

His brother told him to do the chicken dance.

Even his loyal dog, Max, tried to offer advice, although Timmy couldn't quite understand his barks and wagging tail.

Nothing was working! Timmy was beginning to worry his fart would be stuck forever.

In desperation he called his best friend Jimmy.

"Have you tried telling a joke?" Jimmy asked.

Timmy was skeptical. He wondered exactly how that would help.

Jimmy explained, "Well, maybe your fart needs a good laugh to loosen up and escape!"

Timmy thought it was worth a try.

He took a deep breath and whispered the funniest joke he knew into his tummy.

Suddenly, he felt a slight rumble. Could it be? Was it working?

Then it happened—the trapped fart finally burst forth with a loud, thunderous sound .

"Mom, guess what?" Timmy shouted "I farted!"

"I know" Timmy's Mom called back. "I heard you from here!"

Everyone started laughing.

Until Timmy's sister had to fart...

Thank you to Canva and associates.

Made in the USA
Las Vegas, NV
09 June 2023

73104116R00019